Necker Island

French Frigate Shoals

Nihoa Island

Kaua'i

Ni'ihau

O‘ahu

Moloka'i

Lana'i

Maui

Kaho'olawe

O C E A N

Hawai'i

N
W   E
S

California

DISCOVER HAWAII'S SANDY BEACHES
AND TIDEPOOLS

Written and Illustrated by Katherine Orr

Published and distributed by

ISLAND HERITAGE
P U B L I S H I N G
A DIVISION OF THE MADDEN CORPORATION

Cover and book design by Jui-Lien Fletcher
First edition, Third printing 1998

Please address orders and correspondence to:

ISLAND HERITAGE
99-880 Iwaena Street
Aiea, Hawaii 96701
(808) 487-7299

Printed in Hong Kong

DISCOVER HAWAI'I'S
Sandy beaches & Tidepools

Written and Illustrated by Katherine Orr

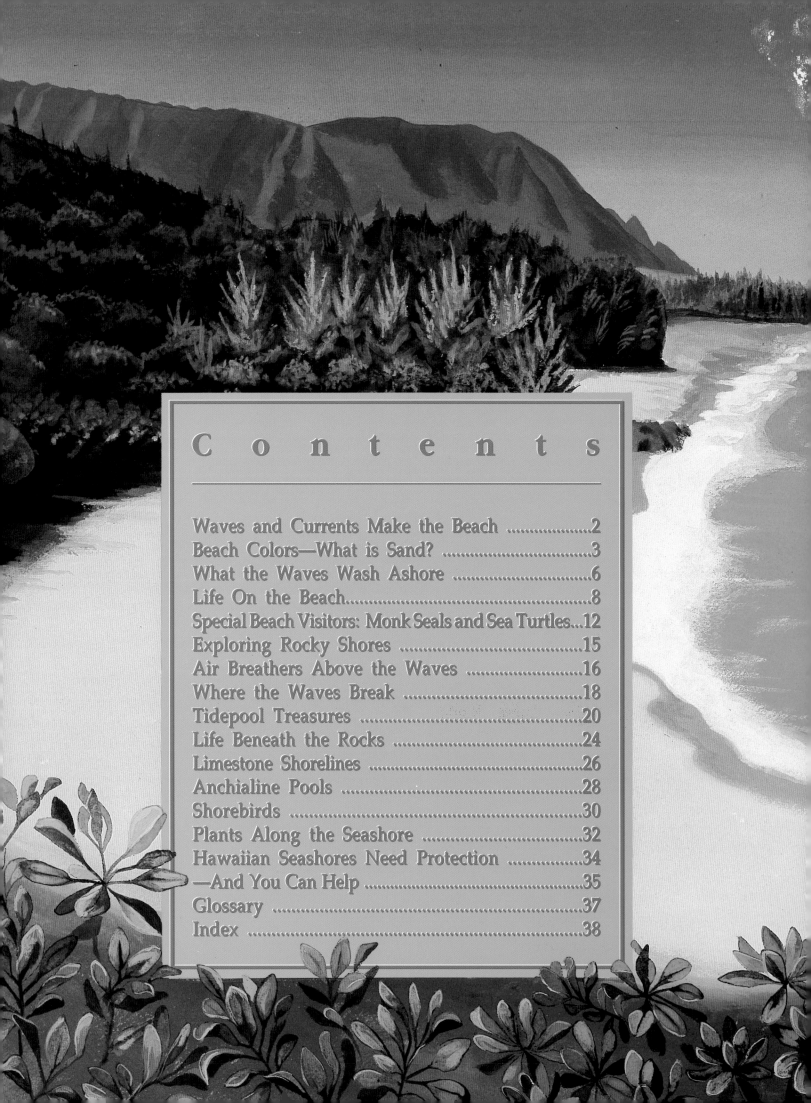

Contents

Hala leaves rustle in the dancing breeze. Waves boom and hiss as they break against the shore. Between trees and waves the shoreline lies silent. The black rocks and bright beaches look lifeless and still, but are they really? Walk along the warm beach and find out what lives within this shifting, changing world of sand. Peer into rocky tidepools and discover a tiny, busy world in motion. There is mystery and beauty in these special places where life is often small and hidden. Come explore the living seashores of Hawai'i and discover the amazing world where land meets sea.

WAVES AND CURRENTS MAKE THE BEACH

Beaches are full of stories. They can tell you many things about how they were formed, where their sand comes from, what lives hidden within their slopes, and what lives out beyond the breaking waves.

Look at the size of the sand grains on a beach. Are they large and coarse or are they fine and packed? Does the beach slope gently or sharply toward the water? The slope of the beach and the size of the sand grains depend on the type of wave action along the shore. Large waves pounding an exposed shore create beaches with steep slopes and coarse sand. Gentle waves washing a sheltered shore create gently sloped beaches with fine sand.

Some Hawaiian beaches change their shape and texture with the seasons because the waves and currents that form the beaches are stronger in winter and gentler in summer. Some beaches may look the same throughout the year because an offshore coral reef protects the shoreline from pounding waves.

BEACH COLORS—
WHAT IS SAND?

Most Hawaiian beaches are white, tan, or brownish gray, but some Hawaiian beaches are jet black and others are greenish.

The color of a beach is determined by the color of its sand. Black beaches are made of sand that comes from black volcanic rock. As hot lava flows from an erupting volcano and pours into the sea, the lava cools quickly and explosively producing small grains of volcanic glass and cinders. Waves wash these grains ashore, forming black sand beaches. Nearly all of these very black beaches are found on the island of Hawai'i where Kīlauea, an active volcano, still pours hot lava into the sea.

As black lava rock is exposed to air and rain, it gradually becomes gray or brown. Many of Hawai'i's beaches are made of dark brown and gray sand grains. This sand comes from lava rock that has been broken down by the wind, rain, waves, and rivers.

These sand grains (enlarged) show how a black sand beach changes over time. Newly formed volcanic sand grains are sharp, black, and shiny.

Slowly, waves and weather wear away the sand grain's sharp edges. The grains become smoother. Their color softens into shades of gray and brown.

As coral reefs grow offshore, white sand grains wash ashore and mix with the dark grains. In this way, the beach grows lighter over time.

A beach may appear unchanged, but its sand is always being replaced. Waves constantly bring in new sand and carry away the old. When lava stops flowing to the sea, the supply of fresh black sand stops. Slowly, the black sand turns gray and is joined by other colors of sand from various sources.

The sand on some beaches has a greenish tint. The color comes from grains of **olivine**, a green mineral found in volcanic rock. Grains of olivine and other minerals are washed into the sea by wind and water. Then waves cast them up on the beach as patches of fine, olive-green sand.

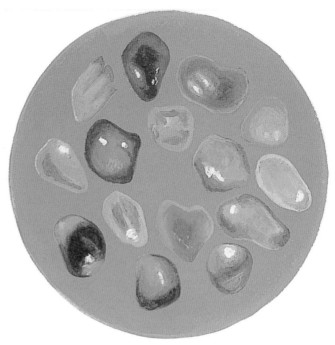

Iron from Hawai'i's red cinder rocks and red clay soils gives some Hawaiian beaches a reddish color, especially after heavy rains.

Hawai'i's whitest beaches are made of sand that comes from the crumbled skeletons of marine animals such as mollusks, crabs, corals, and the skeletons of marine plants called **coralline algae** (COR-a-leen AL-gee). White beaches are usually found near coral reefs where most of these plants and animals live.

Many grains of cream-colored sand are the shells of one-celled animals called foraminiferans (for-am-i-NIF-er-ans). More than a thousand kinds of foraminiferans live in the waters around Hawai'i. Some shells from forams are strung into "paper shell" leis.

Scoop up a handful of white sand and look at it closely. Can you find sea urchin spines, crab claws, and broken bits of rock, coral, coralline algae, and shells? Here are some "puka shells" that are the broken tops of a cone snail's shell. There is the "door" of a turban snail's shell. Most of the plants and animals that produced these skeletons and shells lived on or in the shallow sea bottom, or along nearby rocky shores.

Algae

Nuts and seeds

WHAT THE WAVES WASH ASHORE

Walk along the drift-line and see what the waves wash up. You may find nuts and seeds from trees that live along the seashore. The seeds of some shore plants float and are carried by waves to new shorelines where they may sprout and grow. You may find drying seaweed, shells, and chunks of coral thrown ashore by the surf.

On windward beaches after a storm or strong wind, you may find several animals that spend their lives drifting on the ocean. **Goose barnacles**, or *pī'oe*, attach themselves to objects that have been at sea for a long time. Perhaps you can find some barnacles attached to the underside of a fishing float or piece of driftwood.

Watch out for the **Portuguese man-of-war**, or *pa'imalau*. Its tentacles can give you a nasty sting even though it lies dead on the beach. The man-of-war and its relatives, the **by-the-wind**

Sea urchin tests

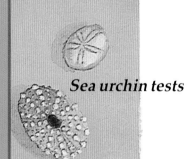

Mollusk shells

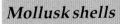

Coralline algae

Coral

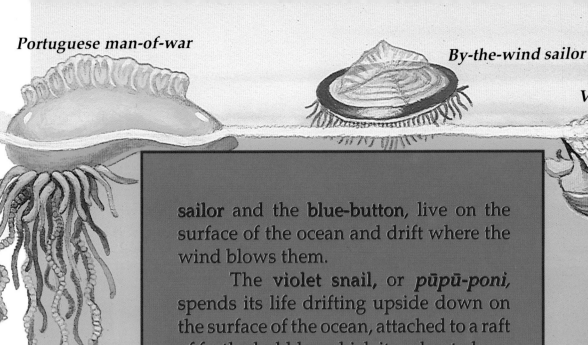

Portuguese man-of-war

By-the-wind sailor

Violet snail

sailor and the **blue-button**, live on the surface of the ocean and drift where the wind blows them.

The **violet snail,** or *pūpū-poni,* spends its life drifting upside down on the surface of the ocean, attached to a raft of frothy bubbles which it makes to keep itself afloat. You may find a violet snail blown ashore, still attached to its raft. Or you may find one clinging to a Portuguese man-of-war or a by-the-wind sailor, its favorite foods.

A small, blue sea slug called *Glaucus* lives on the sea surface. The blue sea slug swallows air and the bubble that forms in its stomach keeps it afloat. Like the violet snail, *Glaucus* eats the man-of-war and its stinging relatives without harm. The stinging cells that *Glaucus* swallows collect in the long tips of its body and are used to defend the sea slug against animals that might eat it.

Notice that these drifting animals of the open ocean are blue. Blue helps these creatures blend with the surrounding sea and sky. On the open ocean, blending with one's surroundings is the best way for slow-moving animals to escape the notice of predators such as hungry fish, sea turtles, and sea birds.

Glaucus

Blue-button being eaten by Glaucus

Goose barnacles

Each plant and animal washed up on the beach has its own story of where and how it lived. But are there any *living* creatures here? At first glance, the beach looks deserted and void of life. On the sand's surface, there is little shelter from the hot sun and nowhere to hide from predators. Churning sand and swirling waves provide no stable ground to attach to. Even food must come from elsewhere, brought in by waves. What could live in such a difficult place?

Just as you wonder about this, you see a quick movement in the wet sand behind a retreating wave. You reach down quickly and uncover a thumb-sized **mole crab**, sometimes called a **sand-turtle**. The mole crab's curved shape and strong hind legs allow it to dig rapidly backwards into the sand until just the tip of its head is showing. A hard shell protects the mole crab from shifting sand as it sits buried at the water's edge, feeding on whatever the waves wash in.

Auger snails, also called **terebrids**, live buried in the sand of some beaches where the waves break. They are active snails with strong shells and muscular feet. Some auger snails move about by letting waves carry them from place to place. Using their foot as a sail, they ride the wave-wash to a new spot and bury themselves quickly into the sand. They remain buried there, feeding on tiny worms, until the next wave comes and they "set sail" again.

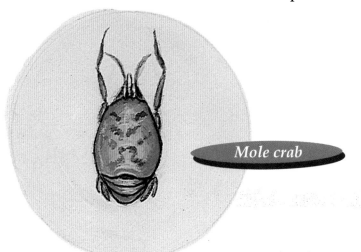

Mole crab

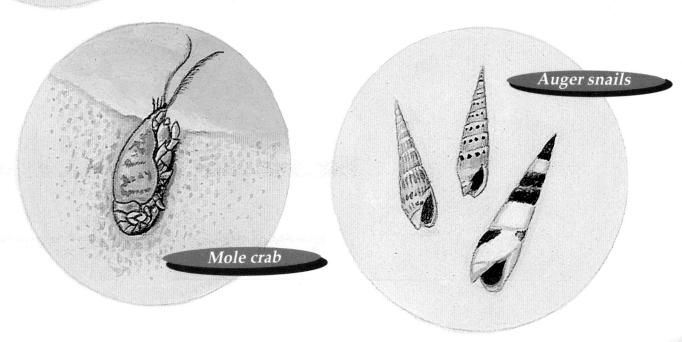

Mole crab

Auger snails

As the afternoon sun sinks lower, the beach comes alive with small, darting **ghost crabs**, also called **sand crabs** or *'ōhiki*. During the heat of the day, 'ōhiki stay hidden in cool, damp burrows beneath the sand. At day's end, they remove sand from the mouths of their burrows and come out to hunt. Each burrow matches the size of the crab that lives within. Some holes are less than an inch across, while the largest holes are about three inches wide.

Like other social animals that live in groups, 'ōhiki have ways of communicating with each other. Adult females and young crabs scatter sand around the openings of their burrows, while adult male crabs pile sand in tall mounds next to their burrows. This lets other crabs know who lives there. Adult males also make a grating sound by rubbing rows of comb-like teeth on the inside of their larger claw against a ridge at the base of the arm.

Ghost crab

Male

Female

Only adult male 'ōhiki have horns above their eyes.

9

A female 'ōhiki carries her developing eggs under her tail. When the eggs are ready to hatch, she releases them into the sea.

Ghost crabs and mole crabs that live on a black beach are dark, while those on a white beach are pale. Over time, these crabs can change color to match the color of the beach on which they live.

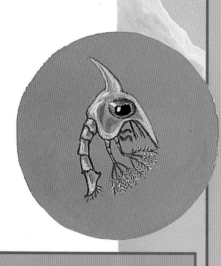

A newly hatched 'ōhiki looks very different from its parents.

With their burrows cleared, the ghost crabs begin to hunt for food—mostly insects and bits of plant and animal matter washed up by the waves. Their swift, sidewards motion and sand-colored bodies make them difficult to see.

Although 'ōhiki live on shore and can breathe air, they must keep their gills damp with seawater in order to breathe. Their offspring must live in the ocean when they are young. A female 'ōhiki carries her developing eggs under her tail. When her young are ready to hatch, she releases them into the sea. There, the newly hatched young drift and grow before coming ashore to begin life on land.

As the 'ōhiki grows, it sheds (ormolts) its crusty outer skeleton and changes form. Soon, this young 'ōhiki will be ready to leave the sea and live on land.

The night is dark and the stars are bright. But wait—there are stars among the breaking waves, and small stars twinkle briefly in the trail of your footsteps as you walk along the wet sand above the breaking waves. Of course these dots of light are not real stars. These lights are made by tiny animals that drift in the sea, called **ostracods**. Ostracods produce light through a chemical reaction called bioluminescence (bi-o-loom-i-NES-ens). Often, the light turns on when these tiny animals bump against a hard object or when waves jostle them. Many small sea animals throughout the world are bioluminescent, including some squids, jellyfish, insects, and single-celled animals. In Hawai'i, small drifting ostracods make most of the wave-washed "starlight" along our beaches.

Ostracods are related to crabs and barnacles. Their small, shrimp-like bodies are hidden between two shells.

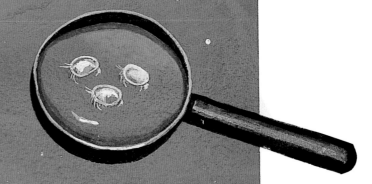

SPECIAL BEACH VISITORS: MONK SEALS AND SEA TURTLES

As you walk along Hawai'i's beaches, you may be lucky enough to see a **Hawaiian monk seal** stretched out on the sand. Hawaiian monk seals are very rare—so rare that they are protected by law. They live only in Hawaiian waters and are mostly found among the uninhabited Northwestern Hawaiian Islands. Monk seals come ashore on quiet beaches to rest and to give birth to their young. Unlike other seals, they do not live in large groups. Since monk seals feed in the ocean at night, they often need to sleep all day on a quiet beach. For their survival, it's best that they are allowed to rest undisturbed.

Often monk seals sleep at the water's edge where the waves gently roll them back and forth. People who see sleeping seals sometimes think they are sick or dying and try to push them into the sea. This is the wrong thing to do. If you see a monk seal on the beach, stay at least 100 feet away from the seal—this is the law.

A summer stroll along one of Hawai'i's beaches between May and September may reveal a strange track that looks like a large tractor tire, running across the beach from dune to sea. This is the track of a sea turtle. Although several kinds of sea turtles live in the oceans around Hawai'i, the most common is the **green sea turtle**. Green sea turtles spend their lives at sea, but come ashore to nest and, occasionally, to lie in the sun.

Since there are so few monk seals and sea turtles left in the world, these animals are protected by law as endangered species—in danger of disappearing from the earth forever.

If you find a seal or sea turtle that you think might be sick or hurt, call the National Marine Fisheries Service or Department of Land and Natural Resources on your island. If you discover sea turtles, turtle eggs, or monk seals being disturbed, captured, or harmed, please call the **Conservation Hotline**. This number works throughout the state. Just dial "O" and ask the operator for "Enterprise 5469."

Highest and lowest tides occur during new and full moons. The greatest height difference between high and low tide in Hawai'i is nearly three feet. The average height difference is about one foot.

EXPLORING ROCKY SHORES

$\mathcal{I}$f you spend much time along the seashore, you have probably noticed that the beach grows wider and narrower during the day. Similarly, rocks along the shore may lie exposed to air for a few hours and then become covered by the sea again. These changes in sea level, called tides, are caused mainly by the moon. As the moon circles the earth, the pull of its gravity on the seawater sets the tides in motion. The tides rise and fall twice in every 24-hour period, rising about 50 minutes later each day.

Changing tides and splashing waves create places along the shore that are sometimes covered by seawater and at other times exposed to air. Animals that live in these areas are exposed to sudden changes in temperature, wetness, and the amount of salt around them. What animals live here? How do they survive? Let us visit a rocky shoreline and see.

Low **tide** is the best time to explore the rocky shore because areas that were covered by seawater at high tide are now exposed to air and are easier to see. Please remember that waves in Hawai'i can be dangerous. While exploring a shoreline, never turn your back to the waves and do not get too close to areas where strong waves are breaking. You may be swept from the rocks and pulled out to sea.

As you discover the hidden wildlife of Hawai'i's rocky shores, remember to be careful and watch where you step. Many animals can be crushed by careless walking.

Animals that live underwater get their oxygen from water instead of from the air. Some animals are harmed by even short exposure to air and can be injured if you lift them from the water. Animals that live on the undersides of rocks will die if the rocks are left overturned. If you turn over a rock to look under it, be sure to put the rock back gently the way you found it.

Every shoreline has its own special plants and animals living there. Please treat them with respect.

AIR BREATHERS ABOVE THE WAVES

Shells dot the rocks above the waves like clusters of small beads. Many are pointed snail shells with fine markings. Closer to the sea but still above the reach of waves and tides are other snails with black, rounded shells. The pointed shells belong to **periwinkle snails**, or *pūpū kōlea*. Both these and the more rounded **nerites**, or *pipipi,* are plentiful on rocks above the waterline. Where sea spray wets the rocks, the snails glide about on their single foot, feeding on a thin layer of marine plants, called **algae** (AL-gee). Pūpū kōlea and pipipi breathe air through wet gills. When the rocks become dry, they pull their shells tightly against the rock and seal off the opening with mucus, or slime. This holds moisture inside the shell and allows them to sit and wait until sea spray returns to their rocky home.

Some snails living along the shore have no gills. They breathe air with a sort of lung, almost as land animals do. Yet, they must live close to the sea because their offspring live in the ocean when they are very young. One such snail is the **false limpet**, or *'opihi 'awa*. When low tide has left the rocks dry, look for these small, ridged shells clamped to the rocks like tiny volcanoes. *Melampus* and several other small snails with lungs instead of gills live hidden beneath the rocks and coral rubble of limestone shores. The living snails are hard to find, but their empty shells are common along some beaches.

The snails on this page all need to breathe air. They will drown if kept under water for too long.

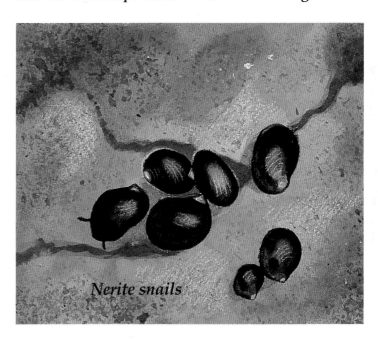

Nerite snails

Pūpū is the Hawaiian word for snail. It also means snack. Pūpū kōlea and pipipi were popular Hawaiian snacks.

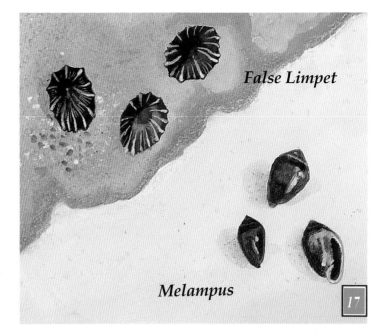

False Limpet

Melampus

17

Red, green, and brown algae grow on the rocks. Some algae are soft and rubbery, others are crisp and hard.

WHERE THE WAVES BREAK

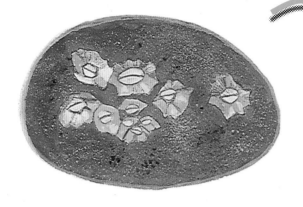

When low tide leaves these **acorn barnacles** dry above the sea, they keep the two "doors" at the top of their shells closed. When high tide covers them with seawater, they extend feathery legs to feed.

'Opihi have long been a favorite Hawaiian food. Hawaiians used 'opihi shells as food bowls and scraping tools.

lgae, or *limu*, grow along the rocks where the waves break. When the falling tide leaves these plants above water, they hold some seawater among their bushy fronds. This provides comfortable shelter and food for tiny snails, crabs, shrimps, and worms.

Among and below the soft algae fronds, the rocks are covered by whitish pink crusts. These crusts are called **coralline algae** because they contain **calcium carbonate**, the same material that coral skeletons are made of.

The incoming waves break and surge against black boulders. Certain animals can live in this churning water because their bodies and shells are designed to withstand the pounding and sucking force of the waves. **Limpets** called 'opihi cling to the rocks with a strong foot and a dome-shaped shell. They glide slowly across the rocks grazing on algae. However, they never move too far from their homes. An 'opihi's home is the place where the limpet has worn away the rock surface in a shallow groove which just fits around the rim of its shell. When an 'opihi clamps its shell tightly against the rock on this spot, it is difficult to dislodge.

Shingle urchins, or *hā'uke'uke,* cling to rocks covered with coralline algae, their food. Unlike other sea urchins, the top of a shingle urchin is almost smooth and its spines are flattened. Long, flat spines around the shingle urchin's sides and strong tube feet help it withstand waves that would pull other sea urchins from the rocks.

Rock crabs, or *'a'ama*, skitter in and out of the surf. Their dark bodies hug the rocks as they pause to nibble algae with their small pincers. Then, quick as a flash, they run toward a breaking wave and disappear beneath the foam. Their flat bodies and long, spreading, spine-covered legs help the rock crabs grip the rock tightly. Like 'opihi and hā'uke'uke, the 'a'ama are designed for life among the breaking waves.

A crab's crusty skeleton does not grow with its body, so it must be shed as the crab grows larger. When a crab's skeleton becomes too tight, it splits along the back and sides. The crab backs out of the old skeleton, already wearing a softer, larger skeleton that formed underneath the old. Within hours, the new skeleton fills out and hardens. The crab scurries away, leaving its old skeleton to bleach in the sun.

TIDEPOOL TREASURES

As the tide drops, the shoreline area becomes wider. Rocks become exposed to air, leaving pools and winding channels of saltwater among the cracks and crevices. Some **tidepools** only receive seawater as spray during very high tides or high waves. They may become very hot and salty in the sun, then suddenly cold and fresh after a rain. There is little life in these pools because few animals can live under such changing conditions.

More animals live in the tidepools that receive new seawater every day. Pools others are very still. With such a variety of conditions, it is not surprising that Hawai'i's tidepools contain a wide and interesting variety of life.

As you look into a tidepool, perhaps the first thing you may notice is a darting fish. Two of the most common tidepool fish are blennies and gobies. Thick lips and tufts above its eyes give a **zebra blenny**, or *pāo'o*, a funny expression. The pāo'o often sits on the bottom with its tail curled, ready to dart quickly. The zebra blenny is sometimes called **puddle jumper** because it can leap from one tidepool to another. The **tidepool**

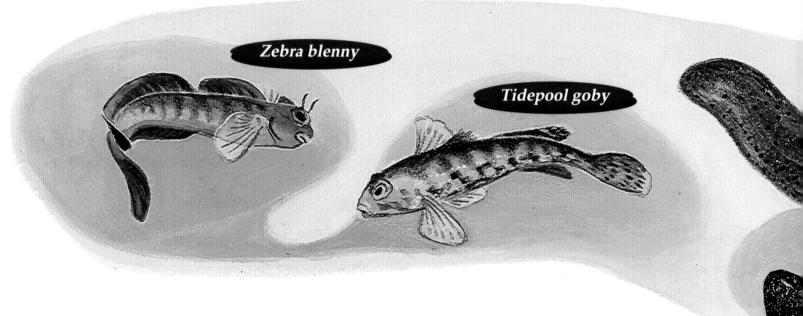

Zebra blenny

Tidepool goby

that are always connected to the ocean usually have the most kinds of plants and animals, because conditions change the least. Some tidepools have sheltered crevices in the rocks, while others have loose rocks sitting on sand. Some pools have waves surging through them, while goby, or *'o'opu ohune*, has a sucker on its underside formed by two fins joined together. It clings onto rocks with this sucker, and often sits at the bottom of the tidepool without moving. When sitting still, the goby is almost invisible because its colors blend with the rocks or sand of the tidepool.

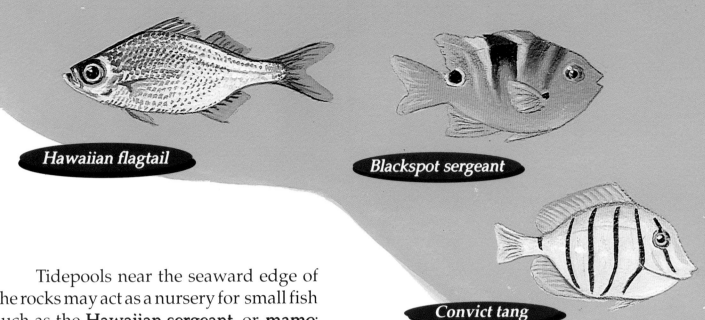

Hawaiian flagtail

Blackspot sergeant

Convict tang

Tidepools near the seaward edge of the rocks may act as a nursery for small fish such as the **Hawaiian sergeant**, or *mamo*; the **blackspot sergeant**, or *kūpīpī*; the **convict tang**, or *manini*; and the **Hawaiian flagtail**, or *āholehole*. Young fish that are small enough to live in tidepools find food and safety from larger fish that might eat them. As the young fish grow older, they move out of the tidepools to the reefs and open shorelines.

Sea cucumbers

You may find **sea cucumbers,** or *loli,* lying on the bottom of a tidepool or in damp sand among rocks left dry at low tide. Some loli have black bodies sprinkled with a thin layer of sand. Others are brown or brown speckled with white. These animals spend much of the time swallowing sand and bits of food that they gather with a ring of tentacles surrounding their mouths. Sea cucumbers are soft to the touch and slow-moving—but they can still be surprising. Do not be frightened if one suddenly shoots out a mass of sticky, white threads as you touch it. This is its way of defending itself. If disturbed, some sea cucumbers will even shoot out some of their internal organs. Fortunately, this loss does not kill the sea cucumber; in time, new organs grow. When handling sea cucumbers, be gentle and refrain from squeezing them; they have no shells or heavy skeletons to protect their delicate organs.

Several kinds of sea urchins live in tidepools. **Boring urchins** with sharp pink or greenish spines are often plentiful in pockets among the rocks. They eat seaweeds which are caught on their spines. They rarely move from their home pocket—a hole which they bore into the rock. The **collector urchin**, or *hāwaʻe,* carries small shells, pebbles, and seaweeds on its short, blackish spines. Do not touch the sharp spines of the **venomous sea urchins** called *wana*. The long, thin, black or banded spines of these urchins break off easily in the flesh. Among the long spines are shorter spines containing poison that produce painful wounds.

Slate-pencil sea urchin

Boring sea urchins

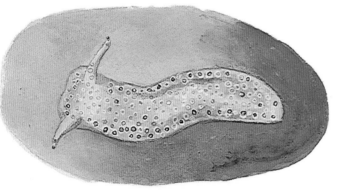

The sea slug, Plakobranchus, eats algae and keeps the algae's chlorophyll within its body. This allows the sea slug to add to its diet by making food from sunlight, just as plants do.

You may discover some unusual snails gliding along the rocks and seaweeds of a tidepool. They are called **sea slugs** because, like garden slugs, they seem to have no shell. Some, in fact, have no shell at all, while others have a tiny shell hidden within folds of skin. Most sea slugs feed on algae.

In some tidepools, small snail shells move around on lively legs. These legs, however, do not belong to snails, but to **hermit crabs**. Although hermit crabs have a hard skeleton on their legs and front ends, their rear ends are soft and need protection. The curled shape

The Spanish dancer is a good swimmer. This sea slug can swim through the water in wave-like motions.

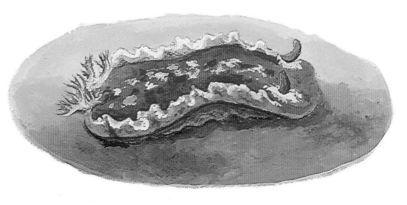

Venomous sea urchin

Collector urchin

spot, attached to the rock by a suction pad at the base of the fleshy body-stalk. One kind of anemone rides around on the back of a hermit crab's shell. When the hermit crab moves into a larger shell, it takes the anemone with it. The hermit crab strokes the anemone until the anemone relaxes its suction grip on the old shell. Then the hermit crab lifts the anemone and places it on the new shell. Scientists think this special relationship helps both animals. Since the hermit crab is a messy eater, the anemone gets an easy meal of leftovers, while stinging cells in the sea anemone's tentacles may help protect the hermit crab from enemies.

of a hermit crab fits perfectly into the coiled inside of an empty snail shell. As the hermit crab grows bigger, it must find a bigger shell to live in. Hermit crabs carry their borrowed shells with them. When disturbed, a hermit crab withdraws into its shell and closes off the opening with its large front claw.

The borrowed shells of some hermit crabs appear to have flowers on them. These "flowers" are animals called **sea anemones** (a-NEM-o-nees). Most kinds of sea anemone live in one

Sea Anemones

Hermit Crab

Hermit Crab

Sea anemones are soft, sack-like animals with a mouth at the top, surrounded by feeding tentacles.

LIFE BENEATH THE ROCKS

As you look into a tidepool you may notice a bunch of white strings, some nearly two feet long, spreading across the bottom from beneath a rock. These are the feeding tentacles of a **spaghetti worm**. The spaghetti worm lives hidden within a tube among the rocks. By stretching out long tentacles, the worm can find food without moving around. Each tentacle has a groove lined with tiny, hair-like structures that move bits of food along the tentacle toward the spaghetti worm's mouth.

Many tidepool animals live on the undersides of rocks, within rock crevices, or beneath rocks resting on a sandy bottom. By gently turning over a rock, you can discover some of them. Please remember, however, that the delicate plants and animals which live attached to rocks will be killed if rocks are left overturned. Rocks that are replaced carelessly may crush the animals beneath them. When you are through looking beneath a rock, always replace it just as you found it.

Once a cone snail finds the animal it chooses to eat, it shoots out a thin dart containing poison that paralyzes the prey so that it can not attack or escape as the cone slowly eats it.

Spaghetti worm

Soft-bodied sea cucumber

Cowry snail

Cone

Pebble crab

Triton

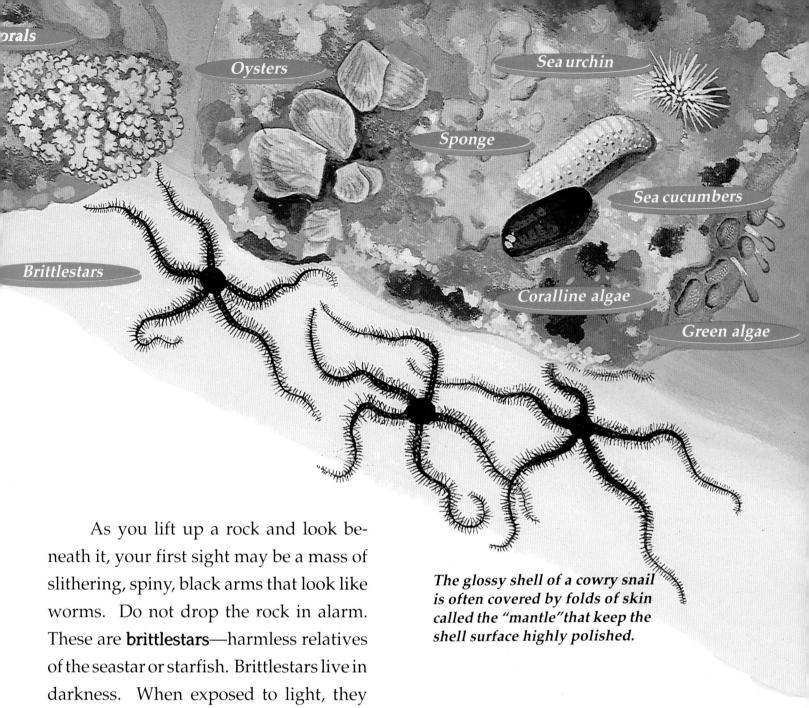

orals

Oysters

Sea urchin

Sponge

Sea cucumbers

Brittlestars

Coralline algae

Green algae

The glossy shell of a cowry snail is often covered by folds of skin called the "mantle" that keep the shell surface highly polished.

As you lift up a rock and look beneath it, your first sight may be a mass of slithering, spiny, black arms that look like worms. Do not drop the rock in alarm. These are **brittlestars**—harmless relatives of the seastar or starfish. Brittlestars live in darkness. When exposed to light, they move quickly to escape it. As the name suggests, brittlestars have arms that break off easily. Luckily for the brittlestar, arms that break off will grow back again.

The underside of a tidepool rock may be brightly colored with coralline algae, green algae, small **oysters** and **sponges**. On the sand beneath a rock you may discover several kinds of crabs, **cone snails**, **cowry snails** or **triton snails**. These crabs and snails rest under rocks and ledges during the day. At night, they come out to feed. Cones and tritons hunt worms, snails, or fish to eat, while most cowry snails eat algae.

Banded coral shrimp

LIMESTONE SHORELINES

Mussels with only the edges of their shells showing may form a living carpet beneath your feet. They attach themselves to the rock with a bunch of tough threads.

Vermetid snails build coiled shells that are cemented to the rocks. Some vermetids live alone. Others live together, forming a living crust that looks almost like the rock itself.

The overlapping plates of a chiton's shell allow it to bend and fit against rocks that are not flat.

On some Hawaiian shorelines, flat platforms of limestone, called **limestone benches,** stretch along the waterline and become partly exposed to air at low tide. Limestone benches occur along seven of the eight main Hawaiian Islands. The island of Hawai'i is still too young to have limestone benches along its shores, but they will develop over time. As you explore a limestone bench, you see coralline algae along the seaward edge facing the waves and thick carpets of bushy algae along the flats exposed at low tide. Some surfaces are covered by mats of small **mussels** and **vermetid snail**, while other surfaces are full of pockets in the rock, each housing a sea urchin.

Look for **chitons** (KY-tons) on exposed rocks at low tide. Chitons cling tightly to the limestone rock, looking almost like part of the rock itself. When covered by seawater, the chiton glides across the rock on its suction foot, feeding on algae.

When exploring a limestone bench think of safety first and remember to watch the waves!

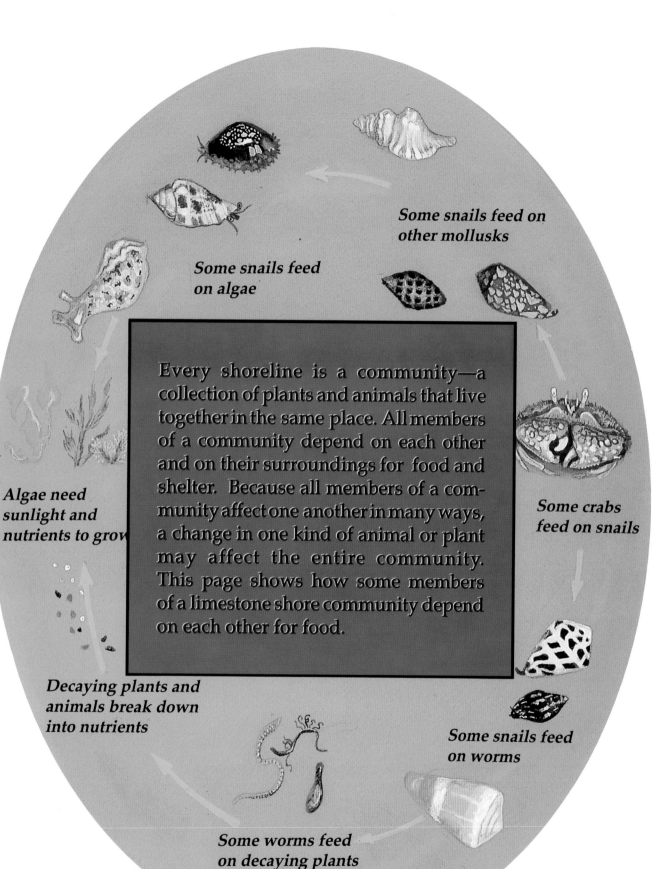

Some snails feed on
other mollusks

Some snails feed
on algae

Algae need
sunlight and
nutrients to grow

Some crabs
feed on snails

Decaying plants and
animals break down
into nutrients

Some snails feed
on worms

Some worms feed
on decaying plants
and animals

Every shoreline is a community—a
collection of plants and animals that live
together in the same place. All members
of a community depend on each other
and on their surroundings for food and
shelter. Because all members of a community affect one another in many ways,
a change in one kind of animal or plant
may affect the entire community.
This page shows how some members
of a limestone shore community depend
on each other for food.

27

ANCHIALINE POOLS

The term **anchialine** (AN-kee-a-leen) comes from the Greek word "anchialos", which means "near the sea." Anchialine pools are found on land near the sea. They contain a mixture of seawater and fresh water that rises and falls with the tides. Fresh water reaches these pools by rainfall and by seepage from higher ground. Seawater flows from the nearby ocean through underground cracks and crevices in the lava rock. There is no surface connection between the pools and the ocean.

Anchialine pools are found scattered throughout the world. Many plants and animals live only in anchialine pool environments. Long ago, the ancestors of these plants and animals were carried inland from the ocean through underground passages. Over many generations, their bodies and habits adapted to life in these pools and also in the dark passageways beneath the ground.

Eleven different kinds of shrimp live in Hawai'i's anchialine pools. Eight of these also live in anchialine pools in other parts of the world, but the remaining three are found only in Hawai'i's pools. In some pools they are so plentiful that, from a distance, the pools look like red clouds. Other pools with small fish seem to have no shrimp, perhaps because the fish eat them. Like ocean tidepools, no two pools are exactly alike.

Snails, insects, small fish, worms and sponges are some of the animals that make up an anchialine pool community.

In the state of Hawai'i, only the islands of Maui and Hawai'i have anchialine pools. The anchialine pools on Hawai'i's Kona coast are in an area near resort hotels. Their future is threatened by more resort development. The anchialine pools on Maui's leeward coast are protected as part of Hawai'i's first natural area reserve, the 'Āhihi-Kīna'u Reserve.

Most of the shrimp that live in Hawai'i's anchialine pools are red and have poor eyesight. Over many generations of living in underground crevices without light, they have lost the need to see and are nearly blind.

Snails

Worms

Algae

Sanderlings

Ruddy turnstones

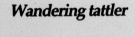

Wandering tattler

SHOREBIRDS

A small flock of **sanderlings,** called *hunakai,* are feeding on the beach. They run back and forth on short, dark legs along the line of wave wash, pecking at small crabs and snails washed in with the surf. Farther down the shoreline, a flock of **ruddy turnstones**, or *'akekeke,* turn over small stones with their bills as they search for food.

A **wandering tattler,** or *'ūlili,* runs along the water's edge, bobbing its tail as it pauses to look around. It is a common visitor to beaches, rocky shores, and stream beds, where it hunts fish and other small animal life for food. As it takes flight, it calls, "too-li-li-li-li."

Sanderlings, ruddy turnstones, wandering tattlers, and golden plovers "migrate," or move from one region to another with the changing seasons. Every April, these birds fly to the Arctic to breed and raise their young. Every August, they return to Hawai'i to spend the winter.

Golden plovers

Pigeons

The **golden plover**, or *kōlea*, is more commonly seen hunting for insects on golf courses, lawns and roadsides than along the seashore. Like the other shorebirds on this page, golden plovers arrive in Hawai'i in August and stay through the winter. In late April, they head north to the Arctic for the summer to breed. By April, the plovers have developed their black and gold breeding plumage which looks quite different from the dull brown colors they wear in winter.

Pigeons, or **rock doves**, are a common sight on many beaches. They come close, begging for food. Please do not feed them. Pigeons were brought to Hawai'i by people and are not native Hawaiian birds. They have replaced native seabirds in some areas and carry diseases that people can catch.

Beach morning glory

Native morning glory

The **beach morning glory**, or *pōhuehue*, sends long, trailing vines across the sand and rocks. In some places it covers the upper beach with a green carpet, splashed here and there with pinkish purple flowers. Roots along the length of each vine help hold the sand in place.

The **native morning glory**, *pā'ū-o-Hi'iaka*, is found only in the Hawaiian Islands. Look for its trailing vines and small purple and white flowers along dry, southwestern seashores.

The **beach 'ilima**, or **'ilima-papa**, grows in a low, spreading mat along the beach. A lei made of the 'ilima's delicate orange-yellow flowers was once the garland of Hawaiian royalty. Each lei took hundreds of blossoms and many hours to make.

Although belonging to the land and not the sea, the plants which border Hawai'i's rocky coasts and beaches are also a part of Hawai'i's living seashores. In order to survive near the ocean, they must be able to live in poor soil with lots of salt, wind, and little rainfall. Unfortunately, many of Hawai'i's native plants have disappeared or become rare as a result of the foreign plants, diseases, and insects that people have brought to Hawai'i and because of human activities on the land. Some native Hawaiian beach plants remain, which are commonly seen along the shore.

Beach 'ilima

Beach spurge

THE SEASHORE

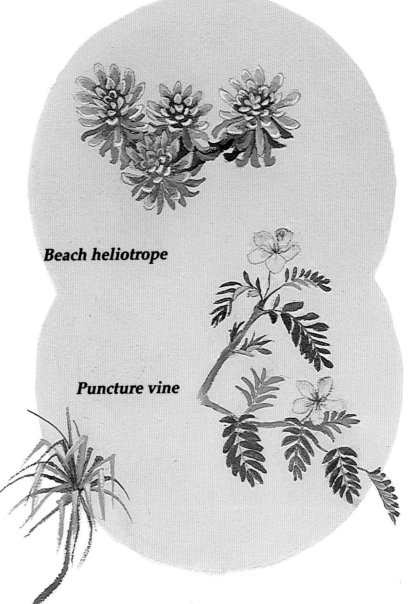

Beach spurge, or **'akoko**, also grows low and mat-like along the coast, often tucked in rocky crevices. Its thick, rounded leaves store water, helping it to live along dry, sunny shores.

The **native beach heliotrope,** or *hinahina*, has another way of coping with harsh surroundings. The silver hairs on its small leaves keep salt and wind away from the leaf, and help keep the plant cool by reflecting the sun's heat.

Like the 'ilima, the **puncture vine,** or **nohu,** is a low plant with yellow flowers; however, its leaves are fern-like instead of heart-shaped. If you see nohu, watch your step. Its tiny fruits have sharp spines which can hurt bare feet.

Beach heliotrope

Puncture vine

Beach naupaka, or *naupaka-kahakai*, is common along many shorelines. The large, green leaves and white berries of this bushy shrub make it easy to spot. Although its small, white flowers appear to have been torn in half, the flowers actually have all their petals.

Pandanus, or *hala*, is the only tree along the shore that may be truly Hawaiian. The male trees have fragrant flowers while the female trees carry large fruits that look similar to pineapples. The Hawaiians used the dried fruit fibers as paint brushes and the hala leaves (*lau hala*) for weaving.

Beach naupaka

Pandanus

Birds get plastic rings stuck around their necks and slowly starve to death.

Fishing nets and lines entangle many forms of ocean wildlife, causing suffering and death.

HAWAIIAN SEASHORES NEED PROTECTION

ven on a remote shoreline you may find rubbish washed up from the sea. It is sad that oceans throughout the world are polluted by plastics, tar, cans, bottles, and other rubbish dumped by people. Some types of rubbish are more harmful than others. Plastic six-pack holders, plastic bags, fishing nets, and fishing lines are especially dangerous and kill many animals every year. If you find these things on the beach, please pick them up and throw them away in garbage cans.

Activities on land threaten seashores as well. Sometimes people dig away the beach by taking sand for use in making concrete. Off-road vehicles, dirt bikes, and motorcycles can tear up and kill rare shoreline plants. Farming and construction of buildings and roads can cause large amounts of soil to wash into the sea. Silt and soil can smother delicate marine life. Chemicals used in farming and on golf courses, gardens, and lawns too often find their way into the sea. Some chemicals are poisons, while others are fertilizers that feed algae. Certain kinds of algae, when given fertilizers, can grow very fast and smother marine life.

DO NOT FEED WILDLIFE...

It seems friendly to feed wildlife, but feeding wild animals can harm them. Wildlife are not designed to eat human food. It may taste good to them, but it isn't good for them. Feeding wildlife turns wild animals into beggars and teaches them to depend on people instead of nature.

Sea turtles eat plastic bags thinking they are jellyfish. The bags plug up the turtles' digestive systems causing the turtles to starve.

—AND YOU CAN HELP

You can help protect Hawai'i's sea shores by:

— taking your rubbish home with you or throwing it in a garbage can;

— picking up rubbish that kills marine animals—such as pieces of fishing nets and lines, plastic bags, and plastic six-pack holders, and throwing it in a garbage can;

—calling the Conservation Hotline number to report sea turtle tracks or a dead or injured turtle, seabird, monk seal, or other marine mammals;

— not feeding birds, fish or other wild animals;

— staying at least 100 feet away from a monk seal on the beach;

—making sure your pet dog or cat does not harm marine wildlife;

— watching your step when you visit tidepools;

— looking or taking pictures, rather than touching; and

— leaving or returning all living animals where you found them.

    The seashores of Hawai'i are like no other seashores in the world. The more we come to know them, the more we want to honor and care for them. We can destroy these living treasures, but we can not create or replace them. The most we can do is protect them by leaving Hawai'i's beaches and tidepools as we found them for future visitors to explore and enjoy.

algae - a group of plants, most of which live in fresh water or salt water. These plants lack true roots, stems, and leaves. Many kinds of algae that live in the sea are commonly called *limu* or *seaweed*.

barnacles - marine animals that form a hard shell and remain attached to a hard surface such as rocks, wood, or fishing floats. They open their shells and extend feathery "legs" which act both as gills and strainers to catch food.

bioluminescence - the creation of visible light by living organisms. Insects such as fireflies, and certain fish, jellyfish, fungi and bacteria, create bioluminescence.

calcium carbonate - calcium is a common element that is found in the earth's crust as well as in most animals and plants. Calcium carbonate is a form of combined calcium and carbon that occurs naturally in limestone, chalk, sea shells, corals, and the skeletons of many small marine animals.

community - groups of plants and animals that live within the same area. All plants and animals in a community interact with one another and affect one another in various ways.

coralline algae - marine plants that form hard skeletons of calcium carbonate. These plants can be pink, red, green or brown, and can form branching or bushy clumps or crusty mats.

environment - the surrounding conditions such as light, wetness, temperature, etc., in which an organism lives.

hala - a tree that grows near moist seashores throughout islands in the Pacific. The leaves are very long and thin with prickly edges, and grow in spiral clusters at the tips of branches. Many stilt-like prop roots help support the tree's trunk near its base.

limestone - a sedimentary rock that is made mostly of calcium carbonate.

marine - something that relates to the sea, that lives in the sea, or that is formed by the sea. *Marine animals* and *marine plants* are animals and plants that live in the sea.

mollusk - the group of saltwater and freshwater animals which includes snails, clams, mussels, sea slugs, squid and octopus.

organism - an individual form of life, such as a plant or an animal.

predator - any organism that lives by catching and feeding on othe living animals.

tide - changes in the surface level of the ocean caused by the pull of the sun and moon as they change their positions in the heavens. *High tide* when the surface level is high, *low tide* when the surface level is low.

tidepool - pools of seawater left trapped among the rocks along the seashore when the tide is low.

I N D E X

Kure Atoll

Midway Islands

Pearl and Hermes Atoll

Laysan Island

Maro Reef

Lisianski Island

Gardner Pinnacles

PACIFIC